Emergent Bloom

Dalvin Williams

Library of Congress Control Number: 2025919221

Published by Hemingway Publishers

Cover design by Hemingway Publishers

ISBN: Printed in the United States

Acknowledgments

I would like to take this moment to express my appreciation to those who have inspired and encouraged me on this journey. Your lessons and guidance have made an indelible impact on my growth and becoming.

To my mom, Cassandra, and my grandma, Charlie Mae—thank you for raising me to be grounded and faithful. You taught me the importance of good morals and an unwavering character.

To my brothers, Von and Duck—thank you for being positive reinforcements in my life. You taught me the things my father could not. You were the guardrails that steered me toward a brighter future.

To my many friends—thank you for being people I can always count on. Always just one call away, you've shown me the true meaning of dependability.

To the love of my life, Asia—thank you for being a positive feedback loop of love, joy, and peace. Your jovial outlook on life continues to inspire me every day.

For my Mom and Grandma

Introduction

In these pages, the author welcomes you on a journey through the elements that help us to grow—*light, soil, and water*. Each section of this collection explores the important sources that mold the human spirit.

With *the light*, poems blossom with love, intimacy, and connection. In *the soil*, roots take hold in the grounding themes of family and upbringing. And through *the water*, the verses meander through sorrow, loss, and pain.

These elements culminate to tell a story of becoming. May you find petals of your flowers in this garden.

Enjoy the bloom

Table of Content

The Light

Picture Perfect

Pictures are worth a thousand words,

so I open my eyes and take a photographic picture of her for my memories.

I put it away in a box labeled "Forever My Love".

On nights when we are apart, I open the box and read the wonders of her smile.

Recite the softness of her lips.

Study the sparkle in her eyes.

There are countless paragraphs of her beauty, and I read them all.

Picture Perfect

Love

How I love you, let me count the ways.

But if I counted how much I love you, I would be counting for days.

And time would pass, and I would age.

And my skin would wrinkle, my hair would gray.

So, let me show you how I love you with the actions I portray,

because my love for you can't be measured with just a simple phrase.

And there's nothing anyone can do, nor anyone can say, that can ever take this love away,

because my love for you will last forever and a day.

Eternal Light

In a flash, you were there, beautiful skin and natural hair.

With sparkling eyes, it's no surprise that our love ignited that night.

In a dark room, you are the candlelight; with infinite wax and wick, you will forever shine bright.

Like a lighthouse, your smile illuminates the way to happiness for lost ones who roam.

Shining with love and peace, you are the way back home,

Your beautiful spirit radiates like the sunshine; you are warm, and you are kind,

I am so glad that I can call you mine.

Eternal Light

Late-night Snack

There's one thing on my mind when it gets late at night,

And that's unwrapping you slowly and holding you tight.

I pick you up and begin to feast as my lips start to glisten.

Moving you closer to me to finish in a more comfortable position.

I roll over after finishing, all tired yet satisfied.

I go to sleep with your taste in my mouth and YOU on my mind.

My fingers will be sticky when the morning comes,

But I'll always enjoy eating my little honey bun.

Warning Sign

When I first met you, your beautiful hair and amazing eyes made you stand out better than the rest.

But above all, what stood out the most was that beautiful yellow sundress.

I was unsure, at first, what the color really meant.

All I knew was that this angel was heaven-sent.

Was it the warm and inviting yellow like the sun on a hot summer day,

or the "DANGER or Warning Ahead" yellow to tell me to stay away?

Nonetheless, I looked upon this beautiful goddess in her yellow sundress and was ready to risk it all.

So I approached to give her my number and say I'm always down for a call.

She smiled at me and whispered, "Be careful; I can be very dangerous, you know."

I smiled back and said, "I'll be careful, but just be sure to take it slow".

Safe Shores

Escaping the tumultuous tides, she swam closer and closer.

That's when the waves of emotions overtook her, and she landed on the shores of my shoulders.

And there, no longer gasping for air, she felt no urge to retreat.

For in my warm embrace, as I looked in her face, she felt a sense of safety and peace.

And in my arms, as I held her tight,

is where she rested, if only for a night.

Fireflies

As a kid, I loved fireflies. I loved how they moved along the backdrop of the midnight sky.

They looked like two lovers dancing for the very first time, letting their love light the way.

Once, I used a glass jar to capture two fireflies.

Bodies flickering in the night like the flame of a candle, dancing like newlyweds for the very first time.

It only took two days for that flame to dim. Fireflies only flash when they're free, so I let them go.

Holding the carcass of past lovers, I saw an empty jar with nothing but air,

dancing like two lovers for the very last time.

Forbidden Fruit

Standing under that big, old apple tree, she asked, "Are you hungry?"

With soft eyes and a voice that calms, he said, "If I had the choice between a feast of kings or an apple under this tree with you, I would always choose the latter. With you, I am fed and satisfied, and I crave nothing." Staring into each other's eyes, they both giggled and enjoyed the sweet and delicious fruit.

What Comes Next

We know that summer brings rain and winter brings snow,

We know that ponds sit and that rivers flow,

We know that grass is cut and trees grow,

But what comes next, we'll never know.

We know that storms come and that winds blow,

We know that eagles fly high and blue jays fly low,

No matter what we do or where we go,

What comes next, we'll never know.

We know about the tomorrows of yesterday, for we're living in the now,

But what about the tomorrows of today? Well, it's time to find out.

I sit, wait, and think about what my future holds

Because what comes next, I really don't know.

As I put my hand in God's hand as He leads me on,

As I walk this path of life, trying to make it home,

I'll pray to God for better days to show,

Because what comes next, only He knows.

The Soil

Grandma's Prayer

When my grandmother prayed,

The God of heaven listened, the devil trembled, and the angels quickened to hear.

When my grandmother prayed,

The mountains moved, the storm ceased, and the presence of God filled the room.

Her interceding for me when she prayed is how I know that she cared.

That's why I am forever grateful for my Grandmother's prayer.

-     To Grandma

Grandma's Prayer

Memory Care

When loved ones begin to age and need assistance, they come to you.

With healing hands and a heart of love, you come to the rescue.

When hands begin to tremble uncontrollably, and legs are too weak to stand,

You show up with a heart of gold to lend them a helping hand.

When their memory begins to fail them, and their life is in despair,

You show them the love of God with a smile and a prayer.

So, continue to spread joy as you so often do,

And for many years of working in memory care, we say thanks to you.

Dear Miss,

I'm from where there are hot days and humid nights, mosquito bumps and bug bites.

I'm from where the kids drink from the water hose outside.

I'm from where getting sprayed by a water hose in the summer counts as a pool day.

I'm from the café and Candy Lady. From Penny Candy and Now & Laters. Pickled pig feet and icy cups.

I'm from lawn mowing and leaf pile jumping.

I'm from where they say their goodbyes but continue to talk for another hour.

I'm from a "be in before the street lights come on" kinda place,

Where you sit on the front porch and sip sweet tea while watching the cars pass.

Oh, how I have missed you, Miss. But when I last saw you, I could hardly recognize you.

Is it a feeling that I miss? That feeling of belonging and having a place to call home.

You've been different since my grandmother died.

No tea cakes to eat, no smell of food in the air. No Turkey necks, no cornbread, no collard greens.

Had you changed, or had I?

Your air—not as sweet; your sound—not as joyful.

No kids running, no jumping, and no playing.

No family cookouts filled with laughter and stories.

A place that once held all the memories of my childhood, now sits empty and desolate.

So, farewell to what was once my home as I journey on a road to create a home of my own.

Dear Miss

Mother Earth

The deed was done, a seed was flung, and the fertilization had begun.

It wasn't to be, so he went free, leaving only my mother, Earth, to look after me.

So it was then that my Mother Earth took the stones of her land and built with her hands this strong young man.

And she loved and protected me, and I remember when she said to me,

"The sun will return after every rain shower," and at times, I cried, but the tears must have been like water,

Because, just like a rose, I sprouted to become this unwilting flower.

And for that, I say thanks to you. You taught me to stand up for what's right and hold on to what's true.

You inspired me to be a man, and for that, I will always love and appreciate you.

- To Mom

24

Mother Earth

Forward March

For Christmas, you wanted toy soldiers and lots of them. Green and tan with feet connected. You always had a connection with soldiers. Platoons of plastic army men filled the house.

Whether playing "fight" with toy soldiers or fighting in wars abroad, you were always fighting—Always a battle to be won, always troops to lead to victory.

I was not surprised when you began leading boys into becoming young men as a coach. Football field, baseball field, battlefield—There is no difference to you. You taught me that we are all marching and fighting for something.

So forward we march into the next battle that life throws at us. And like the soldier you are, continue to lead your troops, your players, and your family to victory.

- To my brother

Forward March

Disk Jockey

A risk-taker from birth, even your arrival into the world was a challenge you couldn't refuse.

Born in the great ice storm of '94, you couldn't pass up on a good story.

You, daredevil of a child, always finding something to jump off of. A house. A railing. A bed.

You hard-hitting football player, my "Eagle Twin."

You, with music always too loud. It's no surprise you became a DJ.

Though tasked with bringing joy to others through music, never forget to SLOW down your own life with the JAMS that make you happy.

Continue to show the world who you R and B proud of every milestone you reach.

Remember to enjoy the *soundtrack* of your life. *Volume* on full blast, *listen* to the *bea*t on your own *drums*.

- To my brother

30

Once Upon a Time

"Granny, tell me a story," I said.

"Once upon a time," she began, "there was a little boy…"

Growing up, my Granny had many stories that she shared with me. I sat for hours asking questions and listening to her speak.

She told me about the Emmitt Till murder, the many marches that MLK Jr. led, how her hands ached from picking cotton, and much more. She told me how it felt to be a mother and a wife.

"Granny," I said, "how does it feel to have this big of a family?"

This family tree has many branches that stretch beyond Mississippi. On these branches, we have preachers, nurses, social workers, and doctors. What a big family tree this is!

She told me, "I asked God to let me live to see my kids have kids, and that'll be enough for me. Well, that has happened already, so I guess my story is not over yet."

***

With so many chapters read, your story is now over. But how amazing it was to hear the stories that you told, how grateful I am to know YOURS:

"Once upon a time, there was a woman working in her garden that sat in front of her home. In that garden, she planted a tree that grew so tall that it could touch the heavens."

I am still a boy with many questions. Tell me, Granny, how large can this tree grow? Tell me just how this story ends.

Once Upon a Time

Words Unspoken

I entered this world like a true son of God because I was chosen.

So weep no longer and hear me now, for these are my words unspoken.

To my cousins, aunts, and uncles, I say thanks for the prayers.

Standing in the gap for me made me know that you truly cared.

To my brothers, I know that I was with you for only a short while,

But keep your heads up and continue to always smile.

Bruh, Bruh, may be gone away today.

But we will meet again someday, and in heaven, we will play.

To my grandmothers, I am sure that you understand

that here, I can laugh, play, run, and dance.

So shed no more tears for me because here I am finally free.

And when I see you again, OH! What great joy it will be.

To my parents, who showed me much love and affection

and did anything they could to ensure my protection.

I am home, and I am gone, but not gone forever.

I had a good life on earth, but this life in heaven is much better.

I know letting go of a beloved son is painful,

But just picture me in heaven, still playing with the angels.

I fought a good fight, and I did my best,

But now it is time for me to take my rest.

I know it is hard losing a son,

But never lose faith in God because His will has been DONE.

Rest in peace, nephews.

The Water

Aching bones

There is a punishment for growing old.

The aches and the pains of an aging body in exchange for more time with loved ones prove it.

Conversely, there is no exchange for dying young, no reward for an early exit—Souls leaving as quickly as they came.

Hardly any time for a memory or two before returning to the great unknown.

Black Angels

As a child, I heard stories of black people who had the power to fly. Stories of how masters had to use shackles and chains to keep the slaves grounded.

Cotton fields with echoes of gospel songs and negro spirituals.

"Two wings to fly away, and the world won't do me no harm."

Slave after slave joined in until they all rose and levitated above the white, puffy plant.

But when the powers disappeared and they could no longer fly, the slaves began to run.

Outrunning the terrible present and hoping to arrive at a new and promising future.

So even now, when little black boys are chased by the red and blue sirens, and the shackles and chains are too heavy to run, and the guns are drawn, and the shots ring out, and the running stops, I imagine my ancestors soaring to freedom.

And right then, I could see it.

I swear I could see it, high above the clouds, black angels in the sky.

Black Angels

Village People

"It takes a village to raise a child," they said.

But what happens when the community we built is scattered about and the love we created is gone?

What happens when sons fight fathers and mothers fight daughters, and there is no peace in the home?

Where do we turn for help when the elders are disconnected from the youth and the teenagers torment the streets with guns?

Neighbors killing one another, creating a separation in the communities—this killed the village.

And when the village died, so did the children. Who's gonna save us from ourselves?

War on Love

She was the calm in the storm,

the rose grown in a barren desert, the peace to the war.

And now that she's gone, I can hear shots ringing in the distance.

His Favorite Toy

"A boy breaks all of his favorite toys," she said while reapplying her makeup.

"The twisted leg on the Power Ranger and the dislocated arm on the GI Joe prove it.

He has an imagination brimming with anger and aggression that leaves his playroom filled with discarded limbs.

The wounded soldier only displays the love he has for his favorites.

Other toys are left with no marks or signs of being played with,

but ME...

You can see by my bruises that I am his favorite.

The swollen lip, the bruised cheek, and the blackened eye all prove that he loves me."

She looked once more into the mirror to finish her makeup before reluctantly returning to the playroom.

His Favorite Toy

Afloat

Drowning in depression,

Lungs filled with water, and I still have enough breath to say, "I love you."

Magician

A magician's best trick is to disappear.

And I will understand that when I reach for you and grasp nothing but air, this is just an illusion.

That I will be amazed when or if you ever return.

Sweet Symphony

I am a violinist.

I run the blade across my wrist, and it makes music.

Red notes drip onto the white sheets below, displaying the songs of my sorrow.

Every stroke of the blade builds up to a crescendo of melodies.

What a beautiful tragedy…

Sweet Symphony

Words Hurt

"Sticks and stones may break my bones, but words can never hurt me."

A tune I remember from school, but I'm a man now, and words do hurt me, too.

Because words can be used like weapons, blasted out like shots from a soldier's selection.

Words can kill, or rather, make a man kill himself.

Because the words hit his flesh, and the wounds healed, but the pain never left.

The words went from his ears to his brain and from his brain to his heart.

And now this man's whole world is torn apart.

So take a breath and take a pause because words can cut,

And the after-effect will leave the scars!!

Strange Fruit

Strange fruit, blood on the leaves.

How haunting it is to see them swaying in the wind as their nectar drips onto the leaves below.

In the winter, the poplar trees are bare and silent, refusing to relinquish the bitter taste of their past.

They are untelling of the things that happened here.

But in the summer, it begins.

Bodies hanging from poplar trees like Christmas ornaments.

But for now, in the quiet of winter, we are safe.

Tonight, in the cold and brisk air, there are no fruits in sight.

Oh, to be home once more.

Ode to the south in winter time.

Fly Black Boy Fly

Black boy born, Black boy cry,

Black boy run.

Black boy gets shot for running; Black boy die;

Black boy fly;

Black boy born again to relive this haunted dream.

Fly Black Boy Fly

Survive

This is the world where only the rich survive;

But I've been broke all my life, and it's a blessing that I'm still alive.

They call me crazy because I got hunger in my heart and fire in my eyes.

It may be because life is hard, but I'm just trying to survive.

So I SURVIVE.

I bear the burden of life while I wipe my sweat.

And I wipe my eyes from the tears of regret.

I gave out my heart until I was heartless.

I guess there's no need to search for treasure in this chest.

But I SURVIVE.

And I put my problems and my family on my shoulders.

And that's why it feels like I'm carrying boulders.

But I gotta keep fighting until this round is over.

And I'm going to run, run while keeping my faith intact.

I'm trying to run, but it seems like there's no end to this race track.

But I SURVIVE!

I survive in spite of it all.

Dangling from the cliff of success, trying best not to fall.

And I have to beat my problems no matter the size.

I guess this is the daily struggle of just trying to survive.

And I SURVIVE!!

Survive

About the Author

Dalvin Williams was born in Beulah, Mississippi, to Cassandra Green. After spending his formative years in Mississippi, he relocated to Memphis, Tennessee, before establishing roots in Houston, Texas. Dalvin discovered a passion for writing poetry at a young age. When he is not writing, he enjoys attending live music performances and spoken word poetry events.

www.ingramcontent.com/pod-product-compliance
Lightning Source LLC
Chambersburg PA
CBHW031235120626
46545CB00003B/1124